T0196878

Praise for Marion Winik

"Winik's voice is so true and clear and compassionate, we're happy to listen to any story she wants to tell."
—*Los Angeles Times Book Review*

"Decidedly unfaint-hearted . . . Marion Winik is resilient, hardy, unfazable."

—*New York Times Book Review*

"The effect of her engaging voice is similar to that of a long phone conversation with an old college friend."
—*San Francisco Chronicle*

"By turns sincere . . . hilarious . . . and brilliant."
—*Austin Chronicle*

"Winik's gift for vivid and even ennobling detail frames this remarkable memoir, moving the reader to cry and to laugh—sometimes both at the same time."
—Kirkus

"A wonderful writer."　　　　—*New York Daily News*

Also by Marion Winik

Above Us Only Sky
Rules for the Unruly
First Comes Love
The Lunch-Box Chronicles
Telling
Boycrazy
Nonstop

The Glen Rock Book of the Dead

THE

Glen Rock Book

OF THE

DEAD

COUNTERPOINT • BERKELEY

The author would like to thank Janice Eidus and
Buddy Nordan for their assistance with this manuscript.

"The VIP Lounge" was also published in the
Massachusetts Review.

The Library of Congress has cataloged
the hardcover edition as follows:

Winik, Marion.
The Glen Rock book of the dead / Marion Winik.
p. cm.
1. Winik, Marion—Anecdotes. 2. Death—Anecdotes.
3. Curiosities and wonders. 4. Glen Rock (N.J.)—
Biography— Anecdotes. I. Title.

CT275.W58463A3 2008
974.9'21044092—dc22
[B]

2008013038

Paperback ISBN: 978-1-58243-634-0

Jacket design by Gerilyn Attebery
Interior design by Gopa & Ted2, Inc.
Printed in the United States of America

COUNTERPOINT
2560 Ninth Street
Suite 318
Berkeley, CA 94710
www.counterpointpress.com

for Ellen

When an elephant dies, its family members engage in intense mourning and burial rituals, conducting weeklong vigils over the body, carefully covering it with earth and brush. They revisit the spot for years afterward, caressing the bones with their trunks, often taking turns rubbing their trunks along the teeth of a skull's lower jaw, the way living elephants do in greeting.

—Charles Siebert

Contents

....

Author's Note

I GOT THE IDEA to make a series of portraits of dead people I have known, or whose lives have touched me in some way, during a workshop taught by the novelist Jane McCafferty in January of 2007. She gave a writing assignment based on Stephen Dunn's lovely poem "Tenderness," in which the narrator remembers a woman he knew long ago.

This made me think of The Jeweler, who had passed through my life decades earlier. I scribbled down some lines about him, his paintings, and his mangos, then recalled the circumstances of his death, about which I had heard secondhand. At the same time, I felt my brain begin to crowd up, as if tickets to a show had just gone on sale and all my ghosts were screeching up at the box office. I flipped to a clean page and started making a list of names. When the workshop ended and I went home to Glen Rock, I was still working on my list. I began to think I could make something like a modern version of Edgar Lee Masters's *Spoon River*

Anthology, except instead of fictional folks from a fictional town, my subjects would be real people and the link between them would be me.

For the next few months, I got up as close to dawn as I could. Already they would be waiting in my head. I'd let one into my office for a few hours and we'd have our little séance. This never seemed morbid or depressing to me. I have lost too many people, I think, to make talking and thinking about them an unpleasant thing to do. My life has been shaped as much by people who are no longer living as by people who are, and perhaps this has been particularly true since I moved, in middle age, to Glen Rock, a quiet place. Writing this book has been a chance to hang out with my friends.

In Mexico, they do something like this on El Día de los Muertos: the Day of the Dead, which is observed on November 1 and 2 every year. On these days, people build altars to their loved ones with pictures and flowers and candles, with the old favorite sodas and books and T-shirts and cigarettes. Then they go to the cemetery and stay all night, praying, singing, drinking, wailing. They tell the sad stories and the noble ones; they eat cookies shaped like skeletons. They celebrate and mourn at once.

Marion Winik
Glen Rock, Pennsylvania
January 2008

The Glen Rock Book of the Dead

The Eye Doctor
d. 1969

MY SISTER AND I had been at sleepaway camp in Milford, Pennsylvania, for almost half of our four-week sentence. Saturday, finally, was Visiting Day, when the parents would pull up to Nah Jee Wah's gates in the family cars with boxes of brownies, packs of Twizzlers, forgotten hairbrushes and sweatshirts, awaited as if crossing the river Styx to visit us in Hades. But the night before, the head counselor came to me in the mess hall. Our mother and father had called. Something had come up; they couldn't make it. What could it be, I thought, what could have gone wrong? I paced the dusty paths around the compound all day, eyeing other children with their parents. We had a funeral to go to, my mother wrote that week in her letter. It was a while before I learned that it was our eye doctor, a friend of the family, who had died.

I come from Nah Jee Wah so pity me, there ain't a decent boy in CLC. And every night at nine they lock the door, I don't know what the hell I ever came here for. Forty years later, our camp song is still stuck in my head, but my mother can only tell me the eye doctor was a classmate of Daddy's from school, his family owned a liquor store in Asbury Park. He was a bachelor, had served in the Army. She doesn't think he was gay. Then she recalls the cause of death was an overdose of medication he took for back pain, perhaps intentional, perhaps not. He was addicted, she says.

Like the flap of a seagull's wing that changes the course of all future weather systems on earth, his death was a cause itself. Before long my sister and I would see another eye doctor, would be sent to a camp we didn't hate as much, one where I ate seventeen pieces of pizza in a contest, was caught stealing another girl's tiny china kitten, was in a production of *Our Town* performed for the parents on Visiting Day. It is remarkable to my mother that I remember the death of the eye doctor at all. Actually it's not much of a memory—his moon face, my pearly eyeglasses, an empty picnic table—but it has turned out to be my job to collect things like that.

The Neighbor
d. 1978

....

HE APPEARED at our bus stop one day in sixth grade
with his blond crew cut and goofy smile. His father
had become principal of the high school, and they'd
bought the mysterious house two doors down from us
in the development. While all the other houses had
flat green lawns or perhaps a single weeping cherry,
this house had so many trees, you could hardly see
the front door. The only member of the family we
really knew was the dog, a huge wooly brown Aire-
dale named Chumleigh who caused great hilarity and
panic whenever he managed to bound away from the
person holding his chain. The boy, on the other hand,
stayed on the leash. Which was short, since his father
was the principal. No, he could not come out to play
Spud. Or ride bikes. Or take bong hits. Not that we
ever asked.

These days, if you want to know a secret, you just turn
on the television. Back then, there were only three
channels and none of them had shows where people

....

who were not professional actors wept and threw chairs at one another. Secrets were simply more secret, which meant rumors were more baroque. For example, people said the reason our music teacher was a little strange was because he had run over his own child playing in leaves in the driveway. It was hard to stop worrying about this. There were huge piles of leaves in those days, particularly in front of our neighbor's house, with all those trees.

My neighbor killed himself in his first year of college. My mother saw it in the paper, and no one else has mentioned it since, nor come up with any further details. How can this be, that we have no idea what happened to this boy, that no one remembers a single conversation with him? Today I found his father's phone number on the Internet, which took about ten seconds, and I called it. I told him that I was thinking about his son. Because our old class is having a reunion, I said, fumbling for an excuse. I heard he died? There was a long pause. He said, yes. He did. Have fun at your reunion.

The Virgin
d. 1977

MARTIMARCANETTI, we used to call them, as if the three boys were a single entity, but Marty had the bad-boy rocker looks, Mark was the easygoing freckle-face, and Eddie, who had been held back a year, had a driver's license and enough whiskers to buy beer. Also tinted prescription aviators, shoulder-length, frizzy '70s hair, and a metallic green Ford Fairlane with plenty of room for my little sister, who was Mark's girlfriend, then Marty's. The unlikely innocent of the group, Eddie, was sweet on her too, but had it even worse for one Trisha Gorsky, a girl with jet-black hair and green eyes who never said a word to him. The four friends used to park in the lot behind the mall and drink six-packs of beer, smoke joints, and maybe take Quaaludes if they were around. The laughter echoing in the dark of the car, the green bottles piling up in the well behind the seat, my sister and Marty making out in the back until the boys up front said okay, get a room.

A night like any other, except my sister wasn't with them, stuck home doing an eleventh-hour social studies project. They shot a game of pool, drank a couple of pitchers with some guys at the bowling alley. Piled into the Fairlane so Eddie could take everybody home. A sprinkle of rain, a shortcut behind the SPCA building in Eatontown, and a head-on collision with another car. Broken arms, shattered glass, no word from Eddie in the front seat. A couple of days later half our high school is staring into an open coffin, wondering if you need tinted aviators and an uncomfortable suit in the afterlife. Just in case, someone slips in a J. Geils album. Mark—now a missionary in Thailand and the father of many children, and still friends with Marty, who's a trucker—remembers they saw Trisha Gorsky at the funeral, her cheeks wet with tears.

The Big Sister
d. 1976

I WENT TO Hebrew school with a delicate redhead
who had two older sisters. While the younger girls
took after their angular, elegant Mama, the eldest had
inherited Papa Bear's body type and, as in my house-
hold, the disappearance of unwanted portions of her
anatomy was a vigorous family project. Whether at the
beach club or Thanksgiving dinner, the mothers who
had chubby daughters always had something to talk
about, new diet plans and weight-loss tips and doctors' names traded over zero-calorie iced coffee whips,
proud reports of sixteen pounds lost in six weeks—
or perhaps a relapse, whispered behind a hand. The
older fat girls were in more serious trouble than I was,
but I knew I would be there soon enough if the diets
did not work. The chins. The arms. The bunched white
tubers of thigh, like feral daikon radishes left too long
to burgeon underground.

There is no good time for a fat girl, but the sixties
and early seventies were particularly hard. One of the

sweetest and most talented, a singer with the voice of a nightingale, would die young from heart failure and be said to have choked on a ham sandwich, as if people couldn't get enough of calling her a pig. Even at a good women's college in New York City like the one my friend's sister went to, I doubt smart girls were any kinder than stupid girls. That morning she struggled into the subway station in her woolen suit and stylishly bobbed hair, carrying her heavy book bag. No one knew, when she toppled in front of a subway car, whether it was because she had eaten only a piece of dry toast since the day before, whether her head was swimming from the don't-eat pills, or whether she just decided to lay that body down. Forty-some years later, it's the skinny girls who are dying. *My Twelve-Grape Diet: A Model Confesses*. If she were here, we could order a pizza and cluck our tongues.

The Painter

d. 1975

AGAIN, AT CAMP, I got a letter. Well, not camp, really; it was a meditation retreat in the mountains near Taos—I was seventeen. There was no phone there, so they had already buried my grandfather at a cemetery in Long Island by the time I heard anything about it. It was not a terrible blow; Papa had had a stroke some years before and had been remote and silent ever since.

He was not a talker in the first place, and he was hell on waitresses, but when we were small, he and my grand-mother doted on my sister and me. They took us out to dinner every Tuesday at Grossman's Deli in Asbury and one time on vacation to Hershey, Pennsylvania. My mother tells how they came over so often, some-times they would show up when we weren't home and just wait. She'd turn the corner and see their car parked in front of the house. Shit, she would say. Her own parents had died before I was born.

My mother says Papa believed his life had been ruined because everything came too easily to him; that's why he never gave my father and his other sons a cent. His childhood did sound glamorous, each brother born on a different continent. One in South Africa, one in England, Papa in Sydney, Australia. But despite the business successes, their father died young after a nervous breakdown, which was the term then for virtually any kind of mental illness. Surely it was that inheritance, not the financial one, behind his stubborn joylessness.

He painted. Not well. But a lot, at least for a few years. The walls of their apartment were hung with rectangular canvases, done predominantly in olive green and black, sometimes with harvest gold or a little blue. Many suggested a fall through outer space, combining abstract arcs and lines with the tumbling silhouette of a long-haired, curvy female figure, sort of like the little nymphet used to illustrate the *Playboy* party jokes page, which I also spent a lot of time studying in my youth. The paintings I remember down to the ridges in the oil paint and the lacquer on the box frames.

The oddball of the group was a potato print, done in his signature colors, modeled after one I had brought home from elementary school. For a long time, my picture hung beside his on the wall. The way he and my grandmother went on, you would have thought I had invented potato prints. Oh, yes, my mother says dryly, you were his favorite. Suddenly I thought this was where it began: my long romantic career among the distant and inaccessible, certain I am the bright little girl who can light up their lives.

The Jeweler

d. 1982

IT WAS 1977, the days of Eden in the city of Austin, Texas. I was living there the summer before my senior year of college in New England, and though I was double-majoring in history and semiotics, I had figured out my true purpose in life, which was to own a frozen yogurt store. Frozen yogurt was new; I was an early and passionate convert. One day, while window-shopping for a location in the university area, I took a flight of stairs behind the Varsity Theater and found him in his tiny jewelry shop, safety glasses strapped to his head, making comets of amethyst and silver.

He was about twenty-five, which was old to me, and looked like a Bavarian elf—pink cheeks, smooth skin, goatee and thin ponytail. I explained about my frozen yogurt store. Have you ever had vanilla ice cream with fresh mangoes? he asked. He made it for me after an Indian dinner in his apartment: the first time I had a pappadum, the first time I visited someone whose canvases were stacked against their unfinished walls.

A burning draft card, purple comets in oil-crayon galaxies. Oh! I said, I love these, and he gave me three or four. How much he liked me made me nervous.

We didn't stay in touch, and he died before I moved back to Austin in 1983. He went through a crazy time, I heard, cocaine and strippers at the Yellow Rose, and just when people had almost given up on him he met a wonderful girl. She spoke six languages. Her whole family loved him. Their wedding was practically an affair of state, with limousines full of flowers and diplomats strung down the road. Lady Bird Johnson, even. A month later he slipped out of their bed for a few hours to visit his old friends; when his new wife woke up in the morning he was dead beside her: a cocaine heart attack. The wedding gifts were still in their boxes and the bluebonnets in bloom when all the fancy people had to come back for the funeral.

Today frozen yogurt is everywhere but I have lost my taste for it, and I also long ago lost one of the Colombian emerald earrings he made for my twenty-first birthday; my mother bought the stones and he set them in little cylinders of gold. The other one I'm wearing right now.

The Carpenter

d. 1993

THAT SAME SUMMER, at a swimming hole in Austin where we were playing backgammon and eating bagels, a couple of cute boys from our home state came up to introduce themselves. One of them, an immigrant Italian barber's son, would become my brother, and not only because he married my sister seven years later.

He was our Dean Moriarty, irresistible, legendary, bossy, and full of ideas. He could build anything, fix anything, and he could talk to dogs. He was the first white person I knew to appreciate hip-hop. He had a union card. He talked like Robert De Niro in *Raging Bull*. He had scholarships to art schools in Kansas City and New York, and he loved Keith Haring and Jean-Michel Basquiat. In Texas he spray-painted the name of my first book on a railroad bridge, and when we moved to New York, zoomed around at night printing the shapes of T-shirts on the walls. He and my sister hopped yachts in Florida, sent postcards from his relatives' town in Italy, shipped home little packages of heroin from Thailand. He was not afraid of needles.

Next to one another, our lives were an object lesson in the class structure of the late twentieth-century East Coast suburb, the Italians versus the Jews. For example, the vast difference in the amount of money and attention devoted to our flat feet, lazy eyes, and crooked teeth, our little talents and our educations. He mocked me for how carefully I divided the phone bill in our communal apartment, which, I had to point out, was furnished entirely through his trash picking. We used to laugh ourselves sick with our version of Sonny and Cher's theme song: Well I don't know if all that's true, but you got me and baby, I got you. Babe. Doo doo doo doo. Fuck you, babe.

Do you remember when it seemed impossible that people as young and strong as this would lie with their heads shaved and their bones sticking out, wearing diapers in St. Vincent's Hospital? The year he died, 1993, was near the peak of the dying, and by the end of the century about a half million American boys, and a few girls, would die of AIDS. Twenty-five million worldwide now. It-was-his-time-he-is-at-peace-he-is-free-from-pain-at-last. Who wants to hear these things? I'd rather take the whole last few years of his life, the addiction, the sickness, the breakup, crumple them up and hide them like a paper full of mistakes you don't want anyone to see. I miss him more, not less, as time goes by.

The Art Star

d. 1990

I MUST HAVE taken the same acid he did at a Grateful Dead concert when we were fifteen, because his drawings look just like what I saw: the writhing, intertwined dancers, the fat black line between good and evil, the undulating burstingness of everything. His whole adorable symbology—the crawling baby, the barking dog, the blowjobs and dolphins, TV sets and serpents, flying saucers, dollar signs, and ticking clocks—made perfect sense to me the moment I saw it. Out the dirty window of an A train stopped at West Fourth Street in 1981. It was like when I read "Howl" for the first time: I felt I'd been waiting to see it, or that I had seen it already, that I just wanted to keep seeing it again. Well, I was in luck about that. Soon he was everywhere.

Six years after he died of AIDS, my mother and I saw a retrospective of Haring's work at a museum in Toronto. There were glass cases of his diaries and comic strips and drawings from when he was a kid.

I was already in tears when I saw his birth date, May 4, 1958, three days before mine. Also that year came Prince and Madonna and Grandmaster Flash, as well as poor crazy Darby Crash, poor crazy Michael Jackson, and poor crazy Nancy Spungen. Also my second husband, the anarchist philosopher-king. It was a Chinese Year of the Dog, and the best minds of our generation were the dog minds, marking, always marking, always wagging our tails, thinking about sex, doing it, no sense of public or private, always wolfing the treats, never ashamed to slice the air with our proud egomaniac bark. Where would pop culture be without us?

The Junkie

d. 1991

IN MY YOUTH I was often told, usually by men, that I talked too much, so it was a relief to finally meet a guy who talked more. He was the son of a Chicano boxer from Texas retired to Pinebrook, New Jersey, the hometown of my future brother-in-law, The Carpenter. Growing up, they called him Bean—because he was Mexican, I reminded my sister the other day. Oh, boys will be boys: first tree houses and mischief, then girls and cigarettes, next roofing jobs and heroin. When we lived in the fifth-floor walkup on West Sixteenth Street, he'd show up at the door with his terrible complexion and boundless enthusiasm, sometimes with dope, sometimes sick, sometimes with his huge, silent friend Chris, sometimes with a matchbook on which he had written a phone number to buy a car, or drawn a diagram of how to grow opium poppies on the windowsill.

Remember how we all loved him despite his being somewhat unlovable? my sister said. I do. Having met him at what was probably the low point of my life, the infamous 1982, I was eager for nonjudgmental companionship, and was particularly transfixed by the way he concentrated on retracting the syringe when helping me shoot up. Together we watched my blood unfurl like fireworks in the clear liquid. I followed him around for a month or so, until he shrugged me off by shacking up with an old high school girlfriend. I was living far away by the time they all started dying. My sister remembers that on the way to his funeral she and her husband stopped at the SPCA. They adopted a blond lab and named it Bean. This was how we were back then, she sighs, meaning drugs flattened everything. On the other hand, when my son was 16 he named the puppy I gave him for Christmas after his dead father, so maybe they were just young.

The Showgirl

d. 1986

NOT UNTIL my sister and I were almost grown up did we know we had a step-grandmother: my mother claimed to have nearly forgotten herself. But then came the phone call, and the story. After her parents divorced each other for the second time and my mother returned to New York after graduating from college, she lived with her strict, short-tempered father in his apartment on West End Avenue. It was a tenuous arrangement and fell apart altogether when his girlfriend, a Rockette from Radio City, moved in, dumping all my mother's clothes out of the closet by way of a wedding announcement. My mother moved down the street to her own mother's apartment, where she lived until she married in 1952. She did not invite her father and his new wife to the ceremony, though she called him afterward from the reception and asked him to come. He didn't, and he died not long after that.

About thirty years later, this mystery stepmother called my mom. She had no family, she was getting older, and, as my mother and her sister decided, she herself had never meant to hurt anyone. She turned out to be a sweet lady, still trim and well turned out, and we took her to my aunt's house in Delaware for Thanksgiving.

When she died, she left us what she had. A pearl necklace for my mother and a diamond ring for my aunt. My sister, a freshly certified accountant, did her estate taxes and cleaned out the apartment. My brother-in-law, the trash king, rolled her TV down the street in a shopping cart. When I came up from Texas for a visit, they took me over to get my share of the hair clips, the hats, and the dozens of gloves: lace, houndstooth, elbow-length, kid, lamé, and leather. Even the kitchen drawers were filled with feminine accessories, except for a couple devoted to take-out menus. For years I wore her zebra-striped wraparound dresses, and my sister still has her little sewing box, packed with thread in a dozen shades of purple. A slip of paper is taped inside with a motto typed in capital letters: TRUST YOUR LIFE TO GOD & LOOK OUT FOR NUMBER ONE.

The Driving Instructor
d. 1985

How MANY POEMS can you write about your father? Maybe one for every day of your life. Your father is the poem inside you when you wake up in the morning, the poem like a spine, shaping how you stand and sit, the poem that's with you on the toilet, at the sink, in front of the coffeepot, the poem that leans back into the driver's seat and spins the steering wheel with one practiced hand. Turn left. Left goddammit. For Christ's sake, learn to drive. Anger, forgiveness, duty, money, jokes, your father is the chairman of all these departments. We used to say, Remember what an asshole he could be, but now we can't remember that anymore. What's left is the assholes we are.

Whole religions were made up so people could see their fathers again, and you don't have to be Jesus or Abraham Lincoln to have your actual biography dwarfed by your never-ending story in other people's heads. A thin gruel of memory thickened with everything that's happened since. Twenty-two years out you can hardly taste the stuff you started with but you just keep stirring, stirring, and putting the spoon in your mouth. Every day there is another thing he never saw: my children, my books, my houses, my aging face, the sweet little dog we have now, the latest morons in Congress and the NFL. The things I learned and the things I never have been able to. My disappointments, which would have disappointed him as well, so I might have hidden them. In dreams my father is sitting at the kitchen table, young and smooth-jawed, looking suspiciously like my teenaged son. The phone rings, he answers it. Hey Daddy, it's me. And look at this, still he gives the phone to my mom.

The Young Uncle
d. 1996

THE FIRST WEDDING I ever went to was the marriage of my mother's much younger half-brother to
my father's cousin. Set in a luxuriant Westchester
backyard in the spring of 1971, the bride wore embroi-
dered Mexican muslin and flowers in her long, shining hair; the groom, sideburns to his chin. Off they
went to their new life running a ski lodge in Stowe,
Vermont, leaving my sister and me dazzled by the
sheer romance of it all.

Since their parents died before my uncle was grown,
my mother and her sisters helped raise my him. He
lived with us for a while between semesters at American University in Washington and when he was on
leave from the service, bringing textbooks and tro-
phies and the smell of aftershave to the spare room
over the garage, in which we would poke around when
he was gone. For Halloween, I wore the jacket and cap
of my father's old Marine Corps uniform and my sister got our uncle's, from the Air Force.

My boisterous, magnetic father commanded quite a bit of attention at home and everywhere else, and my uncle was first among his fans. Even as a little girl I noticed how he started to talk just the way my father did and use his expressions and write in all capital letters and how he loved to say my father's name, and later he had the businesses, and the busyness, the two daughters and the fond, gruff impatience, the fine house and the fancy car, and then he died just as young in just the same way, from the heart.

The Mah Jongg Player

d. 1993

EVERYONE bossed her around: her silent, disapproving, soup-sending-back husband The Painter, her imperious Australian mother-in-law, her two sisters, and all four of her children but particularly my father, her oldest, who treated her with utter impatience and exasperation. Call your mom, my mother would remind him, and when he finally did, you could hear him bellowing for the next ten minutes. She was a talker herself, with a rasp that was the product of a million filterless Chesterfields, effortlessly filling in the paragraphs between my grandfather's monosyllables, running cheery interference around his dour comments. She said *ideer* for idea and *fathuh* for father, and did she tell you about how she dated Richard Rodgers when she was a girl in Manhattan? She did hilarious impressions of her friends at the card table or mah jongg, how every blouse and skirt Betty Becker ever bought sat up and drawled, "Well, hellooo, Betty," when she walked into the store. I'm sure Betty Becker bossed her around too.

She was bulletproof as only a purely sweet person can be, as if she were filled up with the honey she spooned into our mouths at Rosh Hashanah in her apartment, a tradition tailor-made for her and the only one she observed. Except for Johnny Carson, who was her nightly companion, followed by hours of insomnia. Well it's 2:30 A.M. now, so I guess I'll go to bed, reads a letter in her loopy penmanship. A love letter, about how good we are to her and how dear. She had a permanent quality of anticipation, as if something wonderful we had planned was just about to occur, and because she loved us all so much this was true. Even a phone call from my father was something to look forward to, and his death was something there is not a word for. The last time I saw her, dying in the hospital of pancreatic cancer at 83, she was eager to get a peek at my three-month-old son. On the table, she had some chocolate, a bag of pastel mints, a huge wheel of sweetened dried fruit. Take it, sweetie, she said, take it all.

The Queen of New Jersey

d. 1992

MY MOTHER's best friend and longtime golf part-
ner had glistening champagne-colored hair that was
always fixed in a smooth bun, merry blue eyes, and a
way of lowering her voice to a throaty Bette Davis
growl to make comments that would crack you up.
Her handsome, wealthy husband owned racehorses,
Rhodesian ridgebacks, and parking lots; they had a
sprawling house on an expanse of emerald grass over-
looking the ocean, full of paella plates and needlepoint
pillows and every other fine thing. Their two gorgeous
boys played football and ran track, were close as kit-
tens, and like everyone else, worshipped their mother.
Even the housekeeper would have died for her. She
was an excellent cook, and unlike others in her age
group and social class, had a pretty clear idea of what
was going on out there. Sweetie, she said to my mom,
watching my sister and her boyfriend nod out in the
Mexican restaurant, why are your kids always falling
asleep at the dinner table?

As in a fairy tale, everything went horribly wrong. She and her husband were having dinner with my parents when the waiter came to the table with a phone call: their older son had been killed riding his bike on Ocean Avenue. Her husband, a heartless practical joker, left her for another woman, and her younger son married and moved away. The baby girl she had after the accident was still in grade school when the ache in her gut became a swift, untreatable cancer. Though the last time I saw her she was still smiling indulgently at this screwed-up world and its denizens, at the useless macrobiotic advice she was receiving from me. Be good to your mom, she whispered. The next time we went there, the palace was empty except for the housekeeper and the motherless princess, staring numbly at the waves.

The Golf Pro

d. 1981

THOUGH A GOLF CLUB is a hive of activity, a pleasure dome, a Peyton Place, a plantation, a parking lot for helicopters, golf carts, riding mowers, and Jaguars, there is often a sense of solitude when you are out on the course. Among the emerald fairways, the ribbons of oak and maple and cherry, the fluffy banks of pampas grass and pussy willow, the turquoise ponds reflecting geese, even the most overburdened, chased-down person feels he or she has escaped. It is this that helps to balance the aggravations of the game.

My mother weathered my childhood with frequent recourse to that verdant oasis, usually with The Queen of New Jersey and one or two others of their little group of devoted women golfers, and sometimes with a traveling golf pro whom she adored, a debonair Dean Martin in shades and cleats. He came to New Jersey in the summer and went back to Boca in the winter, but what he did for my mother's swing lasted all year.

Recently we were driving to a party in some fancy-shmancy seaside town and came upon a small enclave of unusually modest homes. Oh, look where we are, said my mom. This is where my friend the golf pro grew up. He brought me by once to show me. I could picture the two of them, in a big 1970s car, wearing sunglasses and cardigans, my mother happy and relaxed. He was a big ladies' man, she said.

It was winter, when he was in Florida, that he fell ill. My mother, visiting The Queen at her apartment down there, got word and went to the hospital to say goodbye. At his bedside, they spoke in whispers, like spectators at a golf match, like the rushes at the edge of eighteen.

The Second Cousin
Once Removed

d. 1995

ONE OF THE FIRST of millions of women thrown from the wreck when American marriage lost its brakes around 1970, she was pissed off for the rest of the decade. At least. Left with three girls and not much else by that goniff, that nasal-voiced, hatchet-nosed, Vitalis-slicked putz in golfing attire, goodbye Charlie, she was done with men. An early feminist, a single mother, she wrote for the local paper, made watercolors of the Jersey coast, took photographs of lilies, was friends with the horn player from Spring-steen's band. Interestingly, she was my father's second cousin, a relationship more theoretical than manifest, a bridge of mysterious Loises and Bruces I could never keep straight, but which intrigued me because no other family member showed the faintest tinge of bohemianism, and few others were actually heavy though all talked about weight all the time.

The three girls were pretty and huffish, often in conflict with their big mama in the tent top and red glasses.

Their father sometimes sent for them, randomly, and never without repercussions. Complaints and arguments and fallings-out grew in as naturally as molars and bosoms, and one daughter wasn't even speaking to her the year of her death, another quick cancer, but she herself had had it with being angry by then. She made greeting cards from thick folded paper and photographs of flowers and sent them around.

Perhaps that old Mildred or Fanny in our family tree who passed down our shared affinity for musicians and pasta had this other thing as well: the will to stay afloat in murky waters, what, a little schmutz won't kill you, to make out some small but possible bliss in the distance, a dinner party, an art project, and get out the tape and scissors.

The Publisher
d. 1985

YOU CAN CHANGE people's lives by publishing their poems, and this was a power he wielded with generosity, glee, and occasional madness. Out there in his rock house in the Texas hill country he pasted up his literary quarterly by hand, a tabloid, like the *American Poetry Review* or the *National Enquirer*. In ten-plus years he published everybody from Charles Bukowski to Naomi Shihab Nye, from Judson Jerome to me, twenty-two and sultry-banged in my thrilling appearance on the cover.

So debonair with his shock of prematurely white hair and liquid brown eyes, he drove a blue Dodge pickup, kept goats, had to clear the pool table of the poets of Bangladesh and Buenos Aires to shoot a game with a visitor. A special issue on the magical realism of Nacogdoches was in the works. A can of beer in one hand, a couple of pain pills in the other. His damn back again.

To this day I can clearly conjure his fine, tan skin and the elegant line of his nose, and he was a bit of a flirt, but I was his daughter's age and he was a family man. He might have liked to be worse than he was, but you can't fight your own native goodness. He must have felt, after years of chronic pain and Percodan and surgery that didn't help and a yearlong recovery that only took him back to square one, that there simply was no other way out than the one he took on a backcountry road with a hose from the tailpipe of his Dodge threaded into the window. Otherwise he could never have forsaken all those people who had already received their letters of acceptance for the spring issue.

The Clown

d. 1981

THE DEATH of a lover haunts you differently than any other. The first time I learned this, it was from a boy who hanged himself just a couple of months after our ill-fated coupling in the driveway of the home he shared with his girlfriend and their baby daughter. She was one of my closest friends, ten years older than me, an artist and a playwright, a freethinker and a bit of a pothead. He was winsome and slender, a mime and a clown, his irony and his poker face concealing a hard edge of anger and despair. Their half-assed attempt at an open relationship was partially fueled and deeply complicated by her unquenchable attachment to another guy, a mythologically obese, unhappily married local musician, who would screw up her life thoroughly by the time his basso profundo was silenced by an overdose of pain pills in Oaxaca, where he spent the 1990s hiding from the DEA.

It seems almost ludicrous when I think of it, like a movie with too much foreshadowing: the whiteface,

Also, Dana had alerted me to other points of interest. Among these was the flotation tank he had built in the garage of his cubbyhole of a house on Nueces Street in Austin, also featuring a waterbed, a secret garden of skunkweed, and a black Labrador retriever named Lilly whom he loved with all his heart. When you meet a man who loves dogs but doesn't think much of people, you just know you can slip in between the two categories and find something rare.

With all his hobbies and his crabbiness and his fussy ways, his penny-pinching and his remote-control planes and his gentle heart, the Humanoid would have made a great old man. But he was coming back from a hang-gliding trip in New Mexico when a drunk driver going over 100 miles per hour on the wrong side of a highway made sure he never got the chance.

The Skater

d. 1994

THE THIRD TIME I lost a lover I was 36: it was my first husband, the father of my children, the heart of my heart, a gay ex–figure skater I met at Mardi Gras in 1983, which had started out looking a lot like 1982 but was transformed into something else entirely. He was a beautiful young man, and beautiful things formed effortlessly in his wake: double axels, rosebushes, pale yellow-green cocktails made from Pernod. When I saw him tending bar in the French Quarter, I fell in love with him immediately, as did everyone.

Improbable as it seemed and seems, he loved me back. And so began his remarkable transformation from tank-topped Disco Thing to ponytailed stay-at-home dad. It helped that he was a person who felt no need to make sense of things, that despite his cool affect he was driven purely by emotion. Skater, hairdresser, gardener; lover of wall treatments, Virgin of Guadalupe icons, and synth-pop compilations on cassette tape: yet when you saw him with his little sons, who slept in their baby seats on the floor of the hair salon, there was no doubt as to his true calling.

By the time we got married, we knew he was positive and I wasn't. His old friends were already dying. I wholeheartedly believed we would be spared, but perhaps he did not.

There were six good years and two nightmarish ones, during which we took a fair shot at outdoing the virus in wrecking our own lives. Then there was the day he checked out of the hospice and came home to die. He had lived too long in the valley of the shadow, where time bloats up as if having an allergic reaction to your presence, where a week has a million days.

It made me sick when, just four months after he gave up, better drugs were announced, but I don't know if he would have waited even if he knew. Our brother-in-law, The Carpenter, had sent him postcards from a road he never wanted to see.

Many years later, when they were almost men, I gave his boys the tape he made them before he died, a tape I had listened to once and slipped into a drawer. They sat side by side on the bed, unbearably tall and handsome, one with the recorder on his knees, the other pretending to do something on his laptop. What sports do you play? asks their father, his voice high and soft from the morphine drip. He thinks he's talking to the little guys who just visited him at the hospice. Are you taking good care of Mama? Do you remember the day at Grandmom's when the boat floated away and Daddy had to jump in and save it so we could get home?

Three Lost Boys
d. late 1980s, early 1990s

ONE WAS the snappish waiter at the Morning Call in the French Quarter, the guy who looked like a sailor: wavy gold hair, Aegean eyes, weathered, ruddy skin. Another was his boyfriend, a dignified sort with perfect posture and a trim moustache who cut my hair on a velvet barstool in their little slave-quarter apartment. Some of The Skater's friends dropped him after I appeared on the scene, but these two didn't mind.

Our first whisper of the nightmare ahead of all of us came after we'd moved to Austin and they came to visit, pulling up in our driveway in a clattering jalopy, purportedly stopping to refuel on their way out west. Neither was working anymore, they said, or feeling very well. Both were drinking heavily and stealing pills from the waiter's mother, a frail person they had carted along with them from her home in Lake Charles. With their circumstances and charms so reduced, they quickly outstayed their welcome. Then stayed another month. At least it was the kind of thing that makes a good story. I told it for several years without understanding the bad part wasn't the long distance phone bill, or the coffee cups full of port and Coca-Cola.

Their deaths were old news by the time we heard about them, but by then things had started to make their senseless sense. By then you might be handed an informational pamphlet with charts of mortality rates: rows labeled "Men who have sex with men," "Injection drug users," and "Recipients of blood transfusions." By then bravado was becoming very important.

A few years later, I watched my husband rollerblade through Jackson Square with a third boy from that crowd, a young protégé of a dress designer with a studio on Decatur Street. He had learned from the designer how to hand-paint silk and he made beautiful scarves. So adorable in his cut-off shorts, he was a bit of a liar, a wily Southern climber with a well-defined jaw and thick shiny hair, right out of Tennessee Williams.

Both he and my husband knew who was dead and who was alive, and they both knew which side they were on.

The Photographer

d. 2000

THERE WAS a picture of me in the *Austin Chronicle* in 1988 nursing my infant son at a picnic table in a beer garden with a paper bag over my head, moustachioed drinkers on either side. "Hey forget the titty bar, I think I'll just stay here at La Leche League," the caption read. It was taken by a photographer friend I had asked to do me a favor.

She was a rich lady from Corpus with corkscrew curls, button eyes, and skinny rag doll limbs. She had run away from her husband's ranch at 35 to see the world, or as much of it as you could see from a pretty little house in Austin. Motherhood had taken a lot out of her: one disabled son, the other his father's macho mascot, and all she could do and buy and say would never be enough. Finally it was expensive schools, phone calls, and guilt.

She appeared in our world as a wonderful oddity—dry humor, big accent, rooms full of elegant furniture, real art on the walls, and flourishing plants. Way out past Fredericksburg she had another house she called Wit's End. She found our little cadre of artists and hairdressers just as exotic and amusing as we found her; Yankees! Jews and Italians! Members of the middle class! Though she had a deep appetite for solitude, every once in a while she would throw a party at which her banker friends from Dallas stared at other guests in eyeliner, coming in groups out of the bathroom.

All these people were "cute," and the Mexicans on the East Side were "cute," but the pictures she took of them showed more than that. She was the best student I ever had, her old photography teacher told me, too bad she had so much money or she might have had more drive. The teacher and I had less money but better luck: we lived to meet again under the arch in Washington Square Park and talk about our old friend, who died of cancer in her late fifties. How cute she had been, and how much more than cute as well.

The Bon Vivant

d. 1995

ONE OF THE ASSETS of the man I dated after I was widowed—the restaurant critic at the *Austin Chronicle*—was his best friend, an old college roommate and colleague in the food section. He was the youngest of three boys raised in the swamps of East Texas by a Jewish salesman of women's clothing, and all three emerged from that thicket with elegant Southern manners, true modesty, and rare taste.

Despite his unassuming demeanor, our friend could perform miracles with a foie gras or a pan of Brussels sprouts; he could patiently explain the history of cinema, the work of Philip Roth, Patrick O'Brian, or Belva Plain. He sat at the table with the wine enthusiasts as the St. Emilion swirled in the glass and the adjectives flew. Leather, barnyard, tobacco, soil. He waited. Sipped again. Grapes, he said thoughtfully. I'm getting . . . grapes.

He and my old boyfriend would face the night with a bottle of Bushmills Irish whiskey and a pack of Camels and make it all disappear. You wouldn't think there was that much to say about cauliflower. Oh, but there was.

Then on the morning of his 39th birthday, when we were away in San Francisco, he got up, fed his dog, laid out some clothes, and wrote a quick note. He called the police to alert them so they'd be the first to arrive. Then he went into his backyard and shot himself.

We had been trying to pin him down for weeks on how he wanted to celebrate; finally we understood why he'd been so vague. So how long had he been planning this? Since the morning in Port Arthur thirty years earlier when he'd found his mother's body on the floor of the living room?

As a parent, you mark out the limits of the possible. As a gentleman, you do not complain. When he left us, it was like taking Saturday out of the week or May off the calendar, and yet somehow we had to get used to it. If anyone knew this, it was our friend from Port Arthur. I am sure he was counting on it.

The Counselor
d. 1997

A FEW YEARS after the death of The Carpenter, my sister started dating a much older man, an oddly priggish Vietnam-vet-turned-drug-and-alcohol-abuse-counselor she had met at her twelve-step meetings. I didn't cotton to him much, and was glad when they broke up. Once he was long gone, I wrote something a little condescending about him in an essay, later collected and published in my first book.

Well, guess what. In the meantime he and my sister made up, got married, and had a child. Without actually reading it, he became aware that an essay in my book mentioned him, and he began to recommend it to his drug-and-alcohol-abuse clients. Finally one came back and said, Isn't it kind of weird what your wife's sister wrote about you in her book? So he took a look. There was a showdown between us at the beach club that summer and I admitted that I'd been out of line to write what I had.

My excuses were thin—I thought he would never read it, and I thought he was gone forever—and both turned out to have been nearly true. That winter, with a baby at home and my sister into her second pregnancy, he had a relapse, overdosed, and died. She found him on his office floor. Then a few days later in her mailbox she found something else: a pathetic love letter he had written to another woman, marked RETURN TO SENDER.

The following July, amid much blood and tears, she gave birth to his second son. I stood by, holding her hand, wearing the wristband that said Father, so angry at him that I still feel anger now, after all these years. Her older boy, in particular, has his lips and eyes; sometimes a familiar bemused look crosses his face. I want to say, *Yeah, I'm bemused too, buddy,* but how long do you carry on an argument with a ghost?

The King of the Condo
d. 1998

A LIFELONG animal lover, I was disappointed by The Skater's aversion to pets—then completely taken aback by the kitten he hid in the bathroom on my 29th birthday, a week before my due date. How would I take care of a new baby and a cat? A few days later our baby's heart would stop beating and, as we could eventually stand to joke, that kitten would all but wear the onesies.

We lived in a condominium complex then, and Rocco grew up like a kid in the projects. During the day, he hung out on the wall that bordered the parking lot, authorizing arrivals and departures. He ate and slept at every apartment, had twenty-four-hour access to homes I'd never seen. Many people didn't know whose cat he was, and he probably had at least a dozen names. I once heard a redhead with a briefcase call him Mr. Big.

Moving to a single-family house with a yard was not an upgrade for Rocco, but he tolerated his diminished social position with dignity, as if living in rural exile. He never forgot who he was. In 1998, after exceeding all expectations for cat performance for more than a decade, he suddenly grew very thin and listless. When the woman from the vet told me it was feline HIV, I said, Oh my God. My husband died of AIDS four years ago. Well, ma'am, she replied, he didn't get it from the cat. Ah, I wanted to say, but did the cat get it from him?

Philosophers of justice talk about "moral luck"—the difficulty of assigning blame when the consequences of a single act can be so diverse. Truck driver A and truck driver B take the same route, run the same stop sign, but a child darts out in front of B and dies. B is a murderer; A is not. A cat doesn't have to worry about this. Nobody thinks it's his fault he got AIDS, or that anyone else got AIDS.

The people who took care of Rocco while I was house hunting in Pennsylvania expected him to die every day I was gone. But he waited, literally dragging himself to the door on my return.

The Texan

d. 1999

HE HAD THREE siblings and all were his twins, in a way: his biological twin, a brother; his spiritual twin, a little sister; and his dark twin, a brother who so lacked the others' gifts of irony and discernment he fit them like yang to yin. The four grew up in the Permian Basin on the western edge of Texas, where the oldest rocks in the world hide deep pockets of oil and gas, a place that sharpens you like a knife with its dry winds and fierce brightness, a place of which the family owned many acres. The children ran in circles and invented games of chance and torture while downstairs their Cajun father drank and their mother made decisions.

There was only one gay bar in town and eventually three of them would know it well; the fourth would drink elsewhere. Anywhere, really. Wherever they went, the dogs waited outside, sleeping on the side-walk with their noses tucked between their hind legs.

I met the Texan in Austin in the early '80s after his little sister came to my poetry reading. She and I became best friends literally overnight, via one eight-hour conversation held in the apartment she shared with him and his boyfriend. The boyfriend was another dog lover, a kid from Kerrville; their relationship, new then, was to endure twenty years. There would be apartments on both coasts with cream-colored leather couches and good kitchen equipment, delicious dinners of rockfish and pistachio, occasional arguments and betrayals, frequent and joyous reconciliations.

During their New York period, the boys acquired a wire-haired fox terrier named George, born in the Bronx. George would inspire the foundation of People for the Aesthetic Treatment of Animals, as well as a wildly successful line of canine jewelry, bedding, bath products, sweaters, and jackets, which still sell like hotcakes on the Internet and everywhere fine pet products are sold.

They would have been a wonderful elderly gay couple, but it seems no elderly gay couples of our generation were allowed. My friend's brother died at 43 in San Francisco a month before the turn of the century. Shortly afterward, his older brother drank himself to death and his twin nearly did. Their little sister wrapped her arms around a border collie and sipped her beer as slowly as she could.

The Democrat

d. 2004

BY THE TIME I took a job at her son's start-up software company in Austin, she was a sweet old lady who wore fuchsia lipstick and pastel muumuus, a proofreader at the shop where we had our printing done. She corrected our errors with deliberateness and calm despite the extreme sense of crisis her son and I were prone to generate in any situation. I knew she loved poetry and music and politics, but I didn't know her in her heyday, when she and her husband were the entire staff of the only newspaper in Marble Falls, Texas. When she wrote press releases for Ralph Yarborough and campaign ditties for Adlai Stevenson and Lyndon Johnson. When they begged her to sing song after song at parties attended by Ann Richards and Billy Lee Brammer and Willie Morris. I didn't know how it was when her husband left, I didn't know why she never married again. And then, gradually, she didn't know these things either.

When she could not think of the word, could not remember the name, could not work, could not be alone, she bore the bewilderment with grace. Though there were times when it was too much. To be lost, surrounded by strangers, everything so wrong and idiotic, sometimes you could just smack them all and run out the door. You wouldn't think there could be so many years of this, that death could be so patient, determined not just to take you but to erase you altogether. Yet one warm spring day in the timeless time after she couldn't recall the names of her children or even that they were her children, those abandoned loves took her out for a walk. She burst into an aria, sang it full throat from beginning to end. Had she ever sung Italian before? Where did she learn opera? She marched on a half step ahead of them, betraying nothing, a smile on her still-red lips. *Bravo, cara mamma, bravissimo!*

The Wunderkind
d. 2005

HE WAS NOT supposed to go home from the hospital, he was not supposed to live past the age of two, certainly he would never finish grammar school. The doctors had never seen a heart so large, so flawed. Operations with little hope of success were performed, and succeeded. Impossible recoveries were predicted, and completed in no time. All bets were off. There are basically two ways to interpret a situation like this: you are the victim of cruel destiny or the unexpected holder of a ticket to ride. He took the ticket and rushed to the station. At nine, had a little enterprise selling coffee to people waiting in line at the Southern California gas pumps. At fourteen, learned the printing business. At fifteen, finished high school. At nineteen, married a hardworking hippie girl with long blond hair.

By the time he moved to Texas to work with us at the software company, this skinny, bespectacled, prematurely bald wisecracker with his permanent smile and insane capacity for labor was a father of three, a computer whiz, an unsinkable buoy in the raging seas of '80s and '90s technodrama. He survived layoffs and buyouts and mergers that flung others into unemployment lines, graduate schools, and ashrams; spun off some cast-aside department of the original company into an independent concern, became the CEO. The wife quit homeschooling and came to work full-time, and so did the neighbors across the street and a dozen of the last survivors clinging to the wreck of the original firm. The pacemaker operation at forty seemed like no big deal. Like the others, it succeeded brilliantly. The sneaky infection afterward probably surprised him least of all.

The Dentist

d. 2000

EVERY HALLOWEEN I think of him because he gave out holographic slap bracelets and bouncy balls instead of candy. My kids actually looked forward to it; they already had ten pounds of sugar in those pillowcases by the time they got to his house.

It was funny to meet someone my age who had become a dentist, a dentist with shoulder-length hair, Hot Tuna on his CD player, a redwood hot tub, unselfconscious '80s-style narcissism spiking the stolid, beleaguered-but-amused demeanor I more often associate with Jewish men of our parents' generation. His prices were high and we had no dental insurance, so we didn't see him professionally, but prices were low in the beauty parlor my husband ran out of our mudroom. Both the dentist and his wife came in. Until she got a little crazy about her highlights, and it turned into something of a catfight. Then it was just him.

After their divorce, the dentist had the kind of sudden insight into his life that requires shiny vehicles and foreign travel. He started a tour company that led motorcycle trips through the Copper Canyon in Mexico, where the Tarahumara run their famous runs and drink their famous beer. God forbid you meet a Mexican driver on one of those roads.

He didn't—it was a white bird, or a black bird, or, depending on whom you believe, not a bird at all that snapped his head back as he came down the mountain into the sun with his twelve-year-old daughter riding behind him. He was killed almost instantly; she was fine. Fine, but 112, because that's how fast you grow up when you are alone on a road in Mexico and your father is dying in a ditch beneath his motorcycle, killed by a white bird. (She, at least, was sure of this.)

One can only hope the rest of her life has continued to unfold like a myth of the Tarahumara: that the hands that were wrapped around her father's waist cannot feel heat or cold, that white birds appear at times of mortal danger, that she receives a visit from her father every year on El Día de los Muertos. That the light from the mountains keeps coming down.

The Second-Grade Teacher

d. 2001

BY THE TIME my older son was in fourth grade and my younger in second, I had come to believe that their birth years had identifiable personalities. As a group, the children of '88 were among the best anyone had seen: polite, friendly, earnest, their backpacks zipped, their smiles bright. Every teacher, every coach, thought so—and would, all the way through their graduation from high school in 2006. The children of 1990, however, were just the opposite, inspiring rue, exasperation, retrenchment, and the invention of new disciplinary measures wherever they went. As the Chinese zodiac tells us, Horses want things their way and they will become aggressive when all else fails.

Because she was pretty and blond and young, I at first took Vince's second-grade teacher for a marshmallow, one of those pushovers whose perfect letterforms and shining teeth and multiple Miss America exclamation points are such a balm to the elementary school soul. But she wasn't much like that at all. She had a formal, almost nineteenth-century quality, a seriousness about phonics and place value, a certain gravity to her bulletin board displays. She signed the reminders sent home with her first initial and last name, C. Green, and that was what I always called her in my head.

By the time she got to Vince, C. Green was at the end of the alphabet and long hours of coming up with encouraging things to say, penned in careful cursive on carbon-paper layers. "Vince has a beautiful spirit and enjoys school. At times moody or negative in contrast to usual good nature. Something of a 'rebel,' for example about Valentine's dress-up. (Where does he get this?)"

After we moved across the country and my children merged into different groups of squeaky-clean '88s and troublemaker '90s, I heard that C. Green had died of breast cancer, leaving young children of her own. It seemed impossible. Aren't elementary school teachers eternal and ageless—like Santa Claus—holding open the heavy steel doors to the future as the babbling river of children runs through and through?

The Realtor

d. 2006

IF YOU LIVE long enough, life sends you plenty of indignities to rise above. Hangovers, cheap workmanship, the faithlessness of men, the death of loved ones, the signs of aging, the vicious pettiness of people when it comes to real estate. You must focus instead on the joy. To sail through life as she did requires a rare combination of high standards, low expectations, and undimmed enthusiasm. A thick, tough, yet beautifully moisturized and preternaturally radiant skin. The first time I saw her at a party, a tiny woman with a big Texas accent and a fine purple wool coat, it was clear she had it all figured out. I asked for her card. It said Realtor, but might as well have been Realist. For many years it remained in my pocket, an ace in the hole.

When we got into so much trouble selling my house, a crazy mess of misunderstandings and buyer's remorse that spawned a lawsuit of Dickensian absurdity, she took it in stride. She knew the exact way to manage these things: big smile, great insurance, leopard-print suit, and high-heeled boots. This was a gal who had twirled flaming batons for Wetumka High. But our day in court would never come, instead a stupid settlement that gave me a permanent rankle in my justice-bone. Ah, let it go, honey, she told me. The house is crooked, you're not. She opened a bottle of wine she and her writer husband had brought back from Europe and we drank it in her cool, leafy backyard. Tell me all about him, she said, meaning the guy I was moving across the country for. She knew there is little that can't be fixed by a glass of Bordeaux and a juicy love story.

If you live long enough, life sends you the indignity you can't rise above: cancer that kills you in three months, with so much pain you could eat your own pillow. Her dapper husband and ancient mama at her bedside in the hospice, praying her out. Ah, honey. I'd rather think of The Realtor as I saw her in Venice, at a good friend's wedding, giggling with her best friend in the ladies' room of a castle, a silver head and an ivory one bent together, still girlish at sixty-some, though both knew how much hurt a woman can bear.

The Competition

d. 2002

WE WERE the same age, we went to the same college, we both wrote for alternative newspapers, and we each, in 1996, published a memoir about our troubles so far. I did heroin, she drank vodka; I had bulimia, she had anorexia; I was widowed, she was in recovery. First I heard of her was when her book arrived on the *New York Times* bestseller list, "a remarkable exercise in self-discovery." Mine was too, sort of, "if you can imagine Edie Sedgwick mutating into Donna Reed." I stared at her author photo—her high, clear forehead, her mane of blond hair. The beginning is terrific, I told people after I'd read it, the stuff about the glasses and the ice cubes and how much she loved to drink, but after she got sober, it was kind of boring. Could you tell those boyfriends apart? My next book was about single motherhood; hers about how much she loved her dog.

When I heard the eulogy on NPR, saw the obituary in the *Times*, I was blindsided. Lung cancer, 42, are you kidding me? Now she was on my mind even more of the time. When I fell in love with a miniature dachshund a couple years later, I finally read her chronicle of interspecies passion, but all I could do about it now was hug my dog. That summer I was back in Providence where we'd both once gone to school. It was June and the students were moving out, their belongings in piles on the sidewalk. There among the stereo speakers and economics texts, I found a miniature Blue's Clues armchair for my daughter and, on the ground beside it, a paperback copy of *Drinking: A Love Story*. I snatched it up and hugged it as if it were written by my sister. The one I never met.

The Quiet Guy
d. 1999

A TRULY HAPPY marriage is much rarer than anyone admits. In fifty years, I've seen no more than four or five. I think the secret is this: you are connoisseurs of each other's faults. The quirks, the glitches, the annoying habits, the obvious complaints that would drive anyone out of their mind in a couple of months only become more precious to you over the years. The in-laws of my first marriage, The Skater's mother and stepfather, were the real McCoy.

She, a little Italian-Catholic ballbuster, and he, the original geek who never said a word. His idea of a good time was to come home from work in the IT department, fix a pitcher of martinis, and crack open the new Tom Clancy. Her idea of a good time was sitting right there beside him. She had a PhD in his likes and dislikes and her greatest pleasure was to display this knowledge. He never drinks more than one cup of coffee in the morning. Or better yet, in first person plural. We love the Joan Baez Christmas album. We go to Disney in the spring.

They had it all figured out—early retirement, the long-awaited, hard-earned twenty years side by side in their A-frame in the Poconos, on the deck of their Marriott timeshare in Hilton Head, in the cocktail lounge of a ship cruising Alaska. And time with their grandsons: right around then, I moved up to Pennsylvania with the boys. But on a golden October evening during a little bus trip down South, he collapsed at a TGI Friday's. They brought his dessert, he asked for the check, and he put his head down. Not the worst way to die, but a cruel way to leave. She paid the bill and took the bus home.

Tell me, where does the doting go? And the bossing? And the right way to cook the steak? How can a house be so much quieter without the quiet? She will never get over it, in fact she wouldn't if she could. Which might be considered something of a consolation by the less perfectly wed.

The Man of Letters

d. 2004

MY DEAREST FRIEND has had extremely bad luck
with men. While some seemed dubious from the
moment you saw them—the uproarious painter who
ordered whole bottles off the bar, the unkempt, para-
noid "filmmaker" in combat fatigues—this guy had a
certain appeal. He was a surrealist poet from outside
Los Angeles, with smooth, California-colored hair, a
feline languor, a good vocabulary, a pack of Marlboro
reds, a gentlemanly addiction to whatever anyone
might have on hand. At the time, my husband had
Vicodin, Klonopin, and sublingual morphine tablets,
so the two became close. Look, here we all are on the
boardwalk in Bradley Beach, New Jersey, the summer
my boys were one and three. The sun is an orange-
brown pill bottle in the sky. Lounging on a bench, the
men squint through the taffy air at little hands wav-
ing from the Ferris wheel.

"The folly of mistaking a paradox for discovery, a met-
aphor for a proof, a torrent of verbiage for a spring of

capital truths and oneself for an oracle, is inborn in us," wrote Paul Valéry, apparently a realist after all. Along these lines is the folly of mistaking a deluded alcoholic kleptomaniac for the love of one's life. He probably had slipped in his own mind from being a good person to a bad person long ago, but we didn't know it until we took him to a weekend-long birthday party near the Big Bend and so many fine lighters and sunglasses disappeared. Back in Brooklyn, he turned violent and she had to call the police to get him out of the apartment. Eventually the pleading, remorseful letters petered out and the next thing she heard he had overdosed in Europe, his head on the desk between a bottle of wine and a baguette of nearly surreal staleness.

The Bad Brother

d. 1984

ON MY SECOND DATE with the man who would become my second husband, which took place partly in a diner in downtown Philadelphia and partly in a hotel room around the corner, he told me about his brothers. Though he started out with just one brother, two years younger, he acquired a couple more when his mom remarried.

Since the older of the two was in jail (and their own mother was in the bin), only the younger one moved in with them at first. This was, he said, something like having Brad Pitt with fetal alcohol syndrome living in your house. This boy smoked every bowl, downed every drink, wrecked every car—like by driving them into the Washington Monument the first day he got them—fucked every girlfriend. He was a hopeless badass idiot, the crown prince of the hopeless badass idiots, and my husband couldn't resist him, no one could. Even if he was ruining your life and screwing your girl and tormenting you through all your formative years, he was doing it with a big toothy movie-star smile, so you might as well move right into his apartment when your parents kicked you out.

His death was the fucking mess to end all fucking messes. It was the day their parents moved from the city to the farmhouse they'd built in the Blue Ridge. He'd been camping down there for months, working on the house with the builder, which was viewed as part of his turning his life around after all. On moving day he showed up in a pickup loaded with their father's hand-built shelving, his records, his wine. He was with a friend from DC, and they were dusted out of their minds, arguing violently in the driveway, in fact they pulled back out without unloading the car.

Fifty yards down the road, the dope-crazed friend shot my husband's stepbrother, pushed him out onto the asphalt, and drove off. Another mile away he slammed into a tree and died as well. This is where my husband found them, his brother motionless, caved in. The first murder in that county since anyone could remember. Typical, says my husband, the old sorrow and rage still knocking wearily around the back of his throat.

What about the stuff in the truck, I asked stupidly, the records and the wine? Oh, he said, we went over to look at it the next day. Everything was ruined.

76 • MARION WINIK

The Little Brother

d. 1991

CAN'T GET ENOUGH of that Sugar Crisp, I was singing in the babaloo Sugar Bear voice as I poured a bowl for our six-year-old daughter. My husband picked up the box and looked it over. This was my brother's favorite cereal, he said. For a while, I thought he was Sugar Bear. So I added Sugar Crisp to the list: chess, fireworks, Lord of the Rings, '80s synth-pop, a deejay booth, an Asian girl, a bottle of champagne or Bombay gin. A gray silk robe in our closet. A certain hospital in Washington, DC.

That night in the diner he told me about this brother, too, this intense, smart, sardonic, elusive little brother, and I could see it was almost like losing a child (you were responsible for them), like losing your parents (they are never the same), like losing your mate (you are alone with the memories). You are not the fair one without the dark one, the loud one without the quiet one, the big one without the little one, so in a way it was like dying yourself.

We have the copy of the Narcotics Anonymous blue book all his friends at rehab signed the day he got out to go to his court appearance. I would like you to leave me a recipe for that secret charisma you have, wrote Wayne. From Candy: I saw a great change in you, you've started to laugh. Back in DC, he immediately went to the neighborhood to score, then to his grandmother's empty apartment to get high. His grandmother was in the hospital and would die herself a few days later.

My husband wonders still if he did it on purpose. If there was no such thing as heroin would he have found some other way to go out at thirty-one? They buried him next to The Bad Brother on their parents' farm, and he and the brother who was left held a two-man twelve-step meeting beside the hole in the ground. Two older brothers as powerless as older brothers have ever been.

Remember the ten-gallon bottle of liquid Demerol he made when he worked at NIH? These legends are nothing but torture now. It is impossible to feel this is not partly your fault.

The Conscientious Objector

d. 2002

ACTUALLY, I always wanted to be a farmer, said the social studies teacher to the English teacher, as she wheeled his chair into the park so they could make out. Ever since I was a boy. The New Hampshire he'd grown up in was what was left of the whole idea of this nation. Straight and true, tough-minded, hard-ass. One day on a country road, he fought his good friend, as boys will sometimes do. Sickened by it, he decided never to fight again. Halfway through college when the war started, studying history, playing lacrosse, he refused the call to kill. Got sent up with the other COs—12,000 out of 34.5 million—for alternative service, a logging camp in Oregon, a road crew in Michigan. Caught polio, spent a year in an iron lung, left in a chair. Twenty-two.

Finished a BA, a master's, became a teacher. Married the crazy wife, adopted sons. Set kids' minds on fire in a high school classroom outside DC. This was the '60s, the '70s, his classroom full of spider plants and coffee cups and the *Tao Te Ching*. They called him by his first name. He taught them to think. Fell in love in the faculty lounge with a divorced mother of two boys: my husband and his little brother. Got it right this time. Retired with her to twenty dream acres in Virginia, a farmer at last. Immediately, senselessly, their boys started dying. And were planted near the fields where he grew asparagus, lettuce, and raspberries, rolling down the row in his hand-controlled, three-wheeled cart. When, near seventy, frailty began to overcome will, he went back to New Hampshire for the white pine he climbed as a boy, and built his coffin. Five years later, two sons laid him in it beside their brothers. Watched over now by handmade dry stone walls, gathered, carried, fitted together, piled stone by stone.

The Last Brother

d. 2006

THE COMMON THEME of the speeches at his funeral, which overflowed down the steps of a picture-book church in Maryland without a single blood relative in attendance, was: I cannot believe he lasted this long. His stepmother, who married his adoptive father when the deceased was just a teenager in prison, said, I never thought he'd be a good man. His stepbrother said, When I met him he was an asshole. His best friend recounted arguments that ran for decades.

His wife of sixteen years—my sister-in-law—sat silent in the first pew, still in shock. They rarely spent a night apart, but she'd been fast asleep at her sister's when his heart clenched up. She could not have done a thing, the doctor said, but that's what they always tell you. They know it will be hard enough in your little condo full of meticulously organized CDs, movies, baseball caps, and mystery novels shelved to the ceiling, keeping out chaos the way the Hoover Dam holds back the Colorado.

By the time I met him, his chaos days were long over, though his tongue was still sharp as a blade. He was a big bald paleface accountant who was the only other guest invited to his little brother's 40th birthday party. He brought the steaks, I brought the coconut-tomatillo soup. He took one look at me and said I was The One, which was both embarrassing and impossibly endearing.

Within a few years he had turned from a fat guy into a skeleton, living on Kools and Pepsi and not taking his diabetes medicine. Driving up from Germantown to watch the Redskins with his little brother. Who buried him alone in the rocky ground of their mother's farm. Three brothers buried the first, two brothers buried the second and also their father, now one brother buries the other and is alone. A dark summer and a terrible season for the Redskins lie ahead. He will dig his hole himself.

The Last Straw

d. 2005

SIX EGGS and a pint of vodka, sure ain't got much to lose, wailed the singer on the CD downstairs. My husband came into our darkened room and threw himself on the bed, his shoulders shaking, crying so hard he couldn't speak. As long as I'd known him, I hadn't seen him shed a tear outside a movie theater. It was a couple of days after Christmas, the first since the last of his brothers died. We'd been down to Germantown to take Jim's widow out to dinner; afterward, back at the apartment, she had us go through the CDs. Take them all, she said, but there were too many. My husband filled a shopping bag with Stevie Ray Vaughan, Steve Earle, Little Feat, and the female blues singers: Sue Foley, Susan Tedeschi, Lou Ann Barton. Two copies of the only album ever made by the little-known Vala Cupp, a tiny redhead with a big voice who toured with John Lee Hooker for fifteen years.

After he stopped in Damascus for a pint of vodka, he was playing the CDs in the car, reminiscing as he rarely has. Music was what we talked about, he said, the only thing we ever really talked about. At home I went up to bed while he sat by the stereo, looking at Vala Cupp on the front of her jewel case. He got on the Internet to see what she was up to. "Ms. Cupp had suffered for years from bipolar disorder and depression," he learned. "Although surrounded by a circle of close friends in Austin and in frequent touch by email and phone with many friends around the nation, she had become increasingly withdrawn." She answered the phone so rarely, her friends often had to call the police to get the door open. So she'd been dead for five days when they found her hanging in the kitchen, her dogs and cat dazed with grief.

The Bad Influence

d. 2005

YOU DON'T WANT your fifteen-year-old son having friends with apartments, friends who are old enough to buy alcohol legally. You will never meet these friends, as I never met this one. I knew his name, Adam, and that was code for every kind of trouble kids can get into in an unchaperoned apartment in Railroad, Pennsylvania. I pictured a place with black lights and Jimi Hendrix posters and a thousand beers soaked into the orange carpet, as if crash pads hadn't changed a bit since I was a girl.

If I called Vince's cell phone and he said, We're at Adam's, I said, Come home right now! After a while, they stopped chilling there, I was told, because his roommate was sick of all the high school kids. Probably sick of driving back and forth to the liquor store.

Oh, this was a crazy day, this ninth of July. I had to go out at 11:30 in the morning to stop my husband on the lawn tractor and tell him his last brother had died.

That afternoon Vince got a call. Adam had drowned in Prettyboy Reservoir, a place they all went swimming every day. He had floundered halfway across and another boy jumped in to help him, not knowing the most basic lifesaving rule. A drowning swimmer will take you down with him—you have to keep your distance, throw him a stick.

The young girl on the cliff, Vince's age, tried to call for help but she had no service. Screaming as she watched them both disappear. We told him to take his jeans off, we told him to leave his sneakers onshore. Did we tell him he had too much to drink, I thought, and I also thought they would not want to swim anymore at Prettyboy. But there is no way in hell that place is dangerous, Vince told me. Don't worry.

The Burning Man

d. 2005

FOR SOME YEARS there was a saint here in the town of Glen Rock, a young house painter with liver cancer. Just a few years earlier he'd been a badass teenage alcoholic, a two-bit dealer. Then he sold dope to a kid who OD'd. His heart on fire, he turned around and never turned back. Long before he learned of the disease that would kill him at 25, he'd taken an oath: if he could help you, he would.

Though he performed his good deeds in the most unassuming way possible, people said his name with a certain awe. So when my son was just fourteen and getting in deeper trouble every day, I sent a message through a mutual friend, as if calling on the local superhero. He showed up in his tune-blasting Honda Accord and took my son to the sushi restaurant, where they ate Hollywood rolls and talked for a while.

One thing he explained that night, my son told me in the car as we drove home from the funeral, is how you know you are in trouble. It is not when you get caught, not when your parents find out, not when the cops come and things fall apart. It's when you are going to hang with your friends, and you realize you are looking forward to the high more than the people. Stop right there. You have already begun to sell your soul: to trade good for easy, real for fast, sharp for blurred, a bad deal you will rush to make again and again.

Just before we went to Paris that summer, we visited him on a hospital bed set up in his parents' living room. He was barely breathing. When he realized who I was, he apologized and said he didn't think he was going to be able to make the house-sitting gig we had discussed. Although he didn't rule it out entirely.

The R.A.

d. 2006

AT THE ART SCHOOL where we taught were many members of what I liked to call the BLT community: girls who wanted to be boys, boys who wanted to be girls, girls who liked girls, boys who liked boys, and some who had transcended gender altogether. One was a photographer, a web designer, the resident assistant in her dorm, the kind who would drag her sister and brother artists from their various morbid pursuits to go outside and ride bikes. Though she was a sturdy sort who wore men's clothes and used a man's nickname, because she was my writing student, I could never look at her without seeing the little girl from Massachusetts who kicked a hole in the door when she got locked out of the house one time, who suspected they liked her girlier sister better. In my husband's class, Logic, which she hated with a passion, she hinted that she just might be able to refute the whole thing.

In her essays, and perhaps in real life, she called her parents by their first names. Old hippies with a messed-up marriage, they got more sympathy from me than they did from the author. It broke my heart when I read those names in her obituary. I imagined Sharon calling Martin in his home halfway across the country in the middle of the night to tell him the universe had thrown their brand-new college graduate from the backseat of a speeding jeep in Cheyenne, Wyoming, where she'd been sleeping peacefully under the starry Western sky. The sister in China, the grandma in Texas, the brother in Concord: their phones were ringing too. I hope one of them found those files on her computer because she had it all written down, and she always turned in two or three more drafts than anyone else in the class.

The Graduate

d. 2006

Because we moved away from Texas before the teen years came roaring in to sweep my sons and their friends away on waves of testosterone, Red Bull, and cheap beer, here he is at eleven: a pale, reedy blond with glasses, doofy and antsy and unfailingly polite, his toothy, elated smile bigger than the rest of him. His mother was younger than most at our semi-yuppie neighborhood elementary; his teenage sister was raising a baby at home. He was named after his dad, whom he resembled not a bit, a big dark-haired Texas farm boy who played basketball with the kids in the driveway. How fiercely my son loved this friend, not because he was so cool or a sports star or had a swimming pool or anything like that, quite the opposite. You should see how much sunscreen he has to wear, my son marveled after a day at the water park. He is the whitest person in the world.

After we moved, they stayed in touch for a while, visited once or twice. Then those waves of change swept my son off to the locker room and his friend into a bit of trouble. He's doing okay, I think, my son told me. He changed schools. The night of his high school graduation, his family had a big party for him. On his way out the door, he told his mom it had been the best day of his life. Sometime around four in the morning his friends thought he'd had enough, and insisted on following him home. But he fooled them. As soon as they left, he backed out of the driveway and made it about a hundred yards before he flipped his car. A week later I watched my son's class line up to get their diplomas on the football field of a Pennsylvania high school. I looked around at the bleachers full of proud, expectant faces. I don't know how the hell we go on, knowing what we know.

The House

d. 2005

IF YOU VISIT the triangular lot at the intersection of Catina and Mouton Streets, you can still see the oak that shaded the sliver of a yard where its owner once gave a bar mitzvah brunch for the son of our mutual friends—and in New Orleans, even a bar mitzvah brunch may have a certain pagan razzmatazz. In the little galley of a kitchen she mixed mimosas, then carried them through the glass-louvered sunroom to the waiting hands of her guests, and we celebrated our clever children and our general good fortune in the extravagant Louisiana spring. The pink house was no more than a cottage, really, yet it pulsed with housely pride, the accomplishment of a single mother born to a teenaged mother in a world where pink cottages are not handed out by the dealer, where you work your way around the board many times and hoard your cash and count your pot and finally land on the corner of Catina and Mouton, where at last you are home.

It was almost three weeks after the storm when the rescuers made it by in a boat and spray painted their rude crossbones on the roof. They found no people and no animals so they left saving nothing. Beneath the murky waters the pink cottage lay like a shipwrecked galleon, kaleidoscopes and perfume bottles bobbing, straps of handbags twisting like seaweed around the legs of chairs, brightly colored sandals and pumps swimming toward the ceiling of the closet like tropical fish. Books swelled, photos slipped from their mounts, bath beads released their oil into the dark gumbo where salt found pepper and Comet and fertilizer and poison. Weeks would go by before she could come back and see the stained and reeking wreck, before she would discover the brave little Christmas ornaments in their plastic lifeboat, the crystal pitcher peeking out of the sludge, blurred pages from an old address book dried brittle as shells.

The Soldier

d. 2007

AFTER WE WATCHED the towers fall, and the phones started working again, and the lists appeared in the paper, and the weeks went by, I realized that I had lost no one I knew: not family, not friend, not friend of friend; not like my sister in North Jersey whose neighborhood was shot through. I was teaching then at an art school in Baltimore and drove down that afternoon to be with the students. One girl's parents worked at the World Trade Center; we were frantic for her all day, but they were spared.

Then many more people died, died in Afghanistan, then Iraq. I didn't know any of them, either. I did not feel lucky, though of course in a way I was.

While my son and I were on our trip visiting colleges, whatever luck this was seemed to run out. We were eating bowls of soup near the Tulane campus when Vince's cell phone rang. A good friend of his had been killed in Iraq. It was a boy I'd liked ever since we moved to Pennsylvania, who at thirteen had kindly attended Vince's ninth birthday party. I saw him not that long ago, Vince said, I gave him hell for enlisting.

Our soup froze, the day cracked, we made calls. People did not know yet, were shocked. Then one friend said, No. I was with him this weekend. He's not in Iraq, and he is not dead.

It turned out that another boy from our high school, a boy with the same last name, had been killed, and someone heard it wrong; this is the rest. Though Vince's older brother had graduated with the young man who did die when his jeep rolled over a home-made bomb in Baqubah, I never met him. When we got home, I read his short obituary: how he ran as fast as a gazelle, how he had so much energy he used to vault the water fountains in the halls of the school.

One boy is alive, another is taken. What kind of luck is that?

The Family Guy
d. 2006

THE BOY was in a coma for several days before he died. He had taken an overdose of his antidepressants, which caused the seizures he was having when his mother found him in his bedroom. The propensity of Wellbutrin to cause seizures is greatly increased in combination with other drugs, so the psychedelic mushrooms were surely a factor. But whether he took the handful of Wellbutrin to relieve the visions produced by the psilocybin or to relieve himself of consciousness permanently is a matter of disagreement among his sister, his mother, and other survivors. A matter of silent disagreement, since who can possibly talk about this?

His sister, a tall dark Semitic-style beauty, was my stepdaughter's best friend. They had brothers the same age, former pipsqueaks now on the way to becoming moody, substance-abusing Jewish teenage boys, the kind I went crazy for back in the day. I watched my stepdaughter press her nails into her hand, talk on her cell phone, lay her head on the table. She watched her friend close up like a mollusk. Then open again, raw and slippery and gray.

In clinical studies, my stepdaughter told me, antidepressants increased the risk of suicidal thinking and behavior in adolescents with depression and other psychiatric disorders. Isn't that like getting pimples from your acne medicine or gaining weight on Slimfast shakes? He had actually stopped taking the Wellbutrin, though, she mentioned, which makes it even more maddeningly unclear what his intention might have been on that April day, after the mushrooms and the *Family Guy* and the spaghetti.

The Baby

d. 1987

····················

I WAS twenty-eight years old when my first baby died. It was a few days before his due date. They never could say why. I held him in my arms once, briefly; he weighed less than a dinner plate. He looked like a little Chinese doll: hair black, eyes slits, skin flushed and not at all corpse-like, fingers curled into fists. We dressed him in pale yellow flannel for his cremation. All the ideas we had about him, even his name, were burned along with his body. The same people came to the memorial as to the shower. My husband started taking sleeping pills in the daytime. I had to wake him up when it was time to try again. The only thing I knew was what I'd learned at my job writing computer manuals: when some mysterious awful thing happens and the whole document disappears, you have to open a new file and start over. That is all you can do. Twenty years later, I don't have any better ideas.

Twenty years later, I was in my kitchen when the phone rang. It was my son, born shortly after the first one. He was calling from his dorm in DC to ask if I had heard about Virginia Tech. I had not, but soon I knew a great deal. For weeks I read about them. I thought about all the things in their rooms and the dates on their calendars. The bridesmaid dresses, the airplane tickets. Their mothers having to wake up day after day to the colorless, white-hot morning, the insides of their heads roaring like houses on fire. One family was pictured in the newspaper the day they drove to Blacksburg to pick up their daughter's body. They brought a favorite dress for her to wear. "I just want to touch her hair," the mother told a reporter. "Her fingers were so little." Don't you see how lucky I was? If I had to lose him, at least it was before I knew him, before all my love poured out of me like milk. At least I could still start over.

The Maid

d. 2006

IT'S EASY to look down on men who pay women to be nice to them, but I believe I had a similar relationship with the lady who came to clean my house on Wednesdays. A big, bosomy, brown-eyed, strawberry blond in a Garfield T-shirt that read "Domestic Goddess," her greatest loves were Jesus and her cat, yet she had a startlingly dry wit and broad mind. And a grown daughter somewhere, an ailing, difficult mother, some bitchy neighbors in the trailer park who complained about her blow-up pool. We talked about these things, and also about how I should switch the rugs in my living room, and she convinced me to buy a dehumidifier for the basement on eBay. All for $16 an hour. When she fell out with another of "her girls," as she called her cleaning clients, over a broken knickknack, I experienced a little moment of sibling victory.

She drove an old white Cadillac that couldn't make it up our driveway in the winter. We begged her to park it at the end and we'd ferry her in the SUV, but driving on the icy hills was terrifying to her—she'd rather walk a quarter mile through the snow in her little white sandals. One day she told me she felt like she was part man inside. I told her I felt just the same way. Then right around Christmas last year, she suddenly started showing up with two helpers. They'd clean the house and she'd sit out in the Caddy. I begged her to come in for a cup of tea. Next time, the helpers showed up alone. Oh, didn't you hear? No, and I could hardly believe she'd had some horrible cancer for which she'd refused treatment and that she'd died alone in that trailer. Since last goddamn week! Didn't she know I would have come in a minute?

The Sikh

d. 2003

IF A PARENT'S NUMBER one worry is that something will happen to her child, number two is: something will happen to me. I will have to leave them when they still need me. Before my work is done. Before I see how they turn out. But in this area, as in so many others, we are not in charge.

The first time I met the big, gruff American man with the turban and the bushy beard, he was working alongside my sister in a small appliance repair shop in the 1970s. Ten years later, I ran into him again, working alongside my friend in the natural foods business. Another few years, and I met his amazing ninety-pound wife: my yoga teacher, then my midwife. By then I had gotten over the fact that they wore those funny outfits and were both called Gurubachan. I was in love with their four children, two sons and two daughters who had Indian names (not, thankfully, Gurubachan). But it took some time to find out their story.

At nineteen, the girl who would become Mrs. G.B. had fled a bad scene in Chicago with her newborn daughter. She wound up in an ashram in Tucson where she found Mr. G.B., a recent college dropout from Baltimore, teaching yoga. By the time her baby turned one they were Sikhs, and they were married. They moved to Topeka, Kansas City, Dallas, and finally to Austin with their growing brood. He was a roofer, a cook, a salesman; she taught knitting and delivered babies; they believed in a life of the spirit and tried to live it every day.

He got a perfect math score on his SAT, their oldest daughter recently wrote me. *He got up every morning at 4 a.m. to meditate and then work on his list, one long, perpetual list of things to do, in a ratty spiral notebook. He once put a down payment on a car with change he had snagged from all of our pockets doing laundry over the course of a year. He didn't cut his hair for 30 years except for the part they had to shave for his brain surgery. The last thing he said to me was, I wish I got there in time to be your birth father.*

She was in her twenties, a mother herself, when multiple sclerosis took his mobility, his serenity, his math skills, his breadwinning, his fatherhood. The ratty notebook was abandoned, empty pages curled, fading items unchecked. Yet he had done what he set out to do.

The Nurse

d. 2007

···

MY SON HAD a friend, a redheaded wraith on a skate-board, who lived with his mother and grandparents. All had the same translucent skin, horsey jaw, and brown dot eyes, and all were medicated beyond belief: the boy for ADHD and oppositional defiance disorder; the older generation for chronic pain, migraines, and depression. Ma and Grandma staggered around the house in their fuzzy pink bathrobes and curlers while Grandpa snoozed in the rocker, waking only when lured by the boy into driving him somewhere. No one said no to the boy; he was the light of their lives. They went to war with the school authorities and the neighbors, they filed suit against the local police. One day they showed up at my door with their crazy eyes and bony hands to tell me to keep my son at home, he was walking the five miles to their house in the middle of the night. My boy is on medication, Ma told me, if he drinks alcohol there will be trouble.

···

Well, she was right. She called me over there one night to pick up my drunken son. I don't know when this happened, I checked their eyes earlier this evening, she said, whipping her penlight out of her pocket. She was a nurse, she explained. It would be weeks before we found out the full extent of the mayhem, and the only time I ever saw her in real clothes was when we all went to court. Afterward I took her advice and kept my boy out of there. How is your old friend? I asked my boy a year later. Oh, he said, it's sad. His grandpa died, his grandma died, and then last month he found his mom facedown in her cereal bowl. I stared at him. Is it possible he is better off now? my son wondered. He is living with his karate teacher. It seems okay.

The VIP Lounge

THE SNIPER'S BULLET, the tunnel wall, the needle, the gas oven: death may be a great equalizer, but the afterlife is another story. If your tragic demise is a defining moment in the history of a generation—so much so that the phrase "defining moment" is invented to describe it—if the children you left behind are emblems of a society of orphans, if you have a postage stamp or are sometimes sighted on an island near the Bermuda Triangle, you will certainly spend eternity behind the velvet rope. At least there you can relax. There Jimi Hendrix looks down Princess Di's dress as she leans over him to tell JFK a story. There Sylvia Plath takes a delicious bite out of Tupac. After Courtney Love, Janis Joplin seems like no trouble to Kurt Cobain. John and George jam with Elvis while they wait for the others. Oh good, here comes Marilyn with a bottle of champagne—if Jim Morrison doesn't get to her first.

Nothing stops it. Not beauty, not humor, not talent, not wisdom. Not youth or health or goodness or fame or love. Not people who need us. Not a job to do. When a beautiful princess dies, everybody knows this all at once, instead of one person crying alone on a cold kitchen floor. What a pleasure it is to grieve in this vast communal way, piling teddy bears and roses at the site of the beautiful corpse, writing poems and watching programs on television for decades to come. To imagine that there is some fairy-tale sense to be made, some reason, some inevitable truth, as if our deaths come from our lives as our voices from our throats. Down the hall, Spalding Gray is telling the story of his suicide to Vincent van Gogh and Anne Frank. It is so good to see them laughing.

Even if I get by the bouncer with a smooth line and a fake ID, it'll be just as awkward seeing them there as it was when we were all alive. Allen Ginsberg won't recall the time I went home with him and Orlovsky after the reading and stayed for a week. Jerry Garcia won't remember whispering Happy Birthday into the microphone during a jam at Englishtown Raceway the day I turned fifteen. But Grace Paley, who defined not a moment but a whole calendar for some passionate young women of the late twentieth century who learned to write by reading her and following her around, if she is there I know she will recognize me, will jump up, arms wide, and say Marion!

About the Author

Marion Winik is the author of five previous books of essays and memoir, and two books of poetry. She has been a commentator on NPR's *All Things Considered* since 1991 and is a contributor to many magazines. She teaches at the University of Baltimore and lives in Glen Rock, Pennsylvania.

Printed in the United States
by Baker & Taylor Publisher Services